D1476964

Peace That Supersedes

Stories, Scripture, and Self Care for Women Dealing with Infertility, Pregnancy Loss, or the Loss of a Child

By: Alexis Harris Oluyole, Maaden Jones, & Sedria Wilson

ISBN: 9781790224296

Dedication

Thank you to my Heavenly Father who is a very present help; healing me daily.
For my first born, Maverick. My forever angel. Mommy loves you and I wanted the world to know how much!
To my husband; best friend; love of my life; Maverick's dad, thank you for always fighting for our love and happiness. You are my air, when life causes me to become breathless. I love you with my whole heart always.
BDL!
-Alexis

All glory to God for being the author and finisher of my story. I dedicate these words to my friend, Alexis. Thank you for inviting me to add my voice to this book, and for your example of grace in the storm.
-Maaden

I humbly and servantly dedicate this book to my Lord and Savior. Without Him, writing this book and having the strength to tell my story would not be possible.

Thank you to my husband for always being right there by my side in all aspects of my life. You have been an amazing contributor to this book and mission. I love you always for it.

To Taylor Jeremiah, my first-born son, may you continue to rest in paradise and look over us all. You are the reason this book was even written. You have made me strong, wise, and prepared to overcome anything that may be deemed impossible. I am thankful and blessed to be your mom.

Thank you to my children Trenton and Sydney. You two are just simply amazing! Always know everything I do is for you both. I love you with all my heart.

To my dear friends and family. Y'all ain't nothing but the truth. Thank you for holding me up when I was weak. Your unwavering support will never be forgotten.

And last but certainly not least, I dedicate this book to all the women who have experienced any sort of issues with infertility, pregnancy and/or child loss. Keep your head up ladies as the road will be easier. Always know I am routing for you and your healing. I am my sister's keeper.

-Sedria

1 Peter 4:12-13 (NLV) - "Dear friends, your faith is going to be tested as if it were going through fire. Do not be surprised at this. Be happy that you are able to share some of the suffering of Christ. When His shining greatness is shown, you will be filled with much joy."

Dear Sister,

If you have decided to pick up this book, that may mean you are experiencing or have experienced a significant lost in your life. My prayer for you as you read this brief memoir is that you will feel a sense of encouragement and hope. When I lost my son, Maverick, I felt like there were literally no words to describe my pain; my grief; my profound feelings of deficit. It felt as though there was now this huge hole in my heart. I had no idea how I should go about repairing it. I am a licensed professional counselor, so ideally, you would think I would seek out a form of counseling during such a traumatic time in my life right? Wrong. It was quite the opposite for me. I had no desire to process my grief in individual therapy or group grief sessions. Don't get me wrong; both outlets are very useful and healthy ways to seek healing!

I just foolishly convinced myself that my experience was too much to share. That is was too painful. I thought no one could truly understand. I didn't want anyone pretending they did or trying to identify with the suffering they knew nothing about. Honestly, I think this is the similar thinking of lots of women. Especially women of color. No matter what our specific reasoning may be, we've somehow convinced ourselves that our stories should be kept tucked away. That perhaps they are 'too much' to share in a mainstream manner. We often find ourselves trying to be strong for others, then we end up baring our burdens alone- suffering privately. As time progressed I continued to seek God through my anger, pain, and healing. It was then that He dropped the idea for this project in my spirit. He spoke to me and helped me to understand that there are many women out there just like me; women of various backgrounds who endure such pains privately. We don't do ourselves or others any justice by keeping quiet, sis!

As I was finalizing this project, I begin to see more influential women speaking up about their experiences and challenges on their journey to motherhood. Women like Gabrielle Union and our former first lady Michelle Obama began to share with the public pieces of their journey to motherhood. I became so encouraged! It gave me confirmation that although I was nervous to share my story (as I am naturally a very private person), I was on the right path. Just as they can be brave enough to come forward to speak their truth, so can we sis! It's our responsibility to share and educate our family, friends, and peers about the challenges that may arise on the path to motherhood. We must not keep quiet any longer! My hope for you as you read this is that you will find a way to connect with other women who are living a similar experience as you. Through our experiences we must use our stories to connect, share, inspire, and encourage one another. In our sharing, our fellow sister can find hope and move toward total healing!

Be encouraged! Be empowered! Be expectant!

With lots of love,

Table of Contents

Prologue

by Alexis Harris Oluyole

Can I ask you a question? When was the last time you felt completely at peace? I mean you felt cool as a cucumber with no worries, free from all anxiety? Considering life's various hurdles, it may not happen as often as you'd like, right? Honestly, how could anyone embody a state of peace while experiencing challenges, setbacks, or devastating circumstances? Moreover, how could God expect us to embody a state of peace in the midst of trial or tribulation? I think we can agree that experiencing 'peace' while also having hurt, pain, or sadness can be somewhat of a tall order, more like an oxymoron.

As believers, we are taught that trials and storms are put in our path to make us strong and steadfast so that our faith may be unwavering. However, when that light drizzle of disappointment turns into a torrential downpour of loss, it's easy to feel yourself set adrift in the elements of the storm. As the going gets tough, more often than not, we are ill-equipped to persevere through the 'toughness' without some form of discontentment. This has a lot to do with our belief system and how we view faith. Many of us have been conditioned to observe faith as a tool that should get us what we want- you know- "the desires of our heart." Faith is rather a strategy for endurance.

Think about how many times have you heard someone reference having "mustard seed" faith as an avenue to being blessed or receiving what you desire from God. Well, this book will visit the other side of "mustard seed" faith. The side of faith that unfortunately isn't often addressed during Sunday morning service. It's the faith that's needed when God flat out says "not now" or simply "no." It's the one that keeps hoping and trusting while feeling crushed, betrayed, defeated, overlooked, or forgotten. This side of faith stretches your limits - and can either pull you to a deeper, intimate level with God or push you to lose your belief in Him altogether.

Peace That Supersedes features what weathering the elements of the storms in life feels like, while navigating it all with a steady faith that enables peace. Whether your storm is loss, grief, deep disappointment, or recurring pain, we hope that by reading this book, your faith will be quickened, your heart healed, and your peace of mind restored.

Here, you will read the personal stories and perspectives of myself and two of my lifelong friends. Joined as spiritual sisters, we have each endured a form of significant loss on our journey to motherhood. Together, we share with you the real emotions that are associated with this hurt and disappointment in the context of a storm. Although God has each of us in different phases of recoupment, we collectively share how God's presence – whether we felt good, bad, or indifferent – kept us anchored as we braced ourselves for heavy winds and the waves of emotions that arise while responding to God's delays and denials.

His Purpose: A Storm is Brewing

Part I by Maaden Jones

My husband stood between his father and best friend under a large oak tree at the end of a long aisle. My own father and I walked slowly and deliberately to meet him flanked by family and friends on either side. Blush-toned blooms and hand-painted scriptures on wooden canvases lining the aisle. Behind me was a vineyard ripe for the September harvest. The sun was shining, the band was playing, and the reception was a non-stop party. It was the best day ever.

A few weeks after returning home from our two-week honeymoon across the Mediterranean, I took a pregnancy test on a whim. I'd never taken one before, but something urged me to just do it. I mean "why not?" Hurriedly and excitedly, I unwrapped the shrink wrap around the pink box, and fumbled with the carton before tearing into the foil package inside to retrieve the test. I sat there on the toilet holding my pee, as I unfolded the little leaflet scanning the English directions to make sure I was doing it right. I mean there's not that much to it, but it wasn't cheap, so I wanted to be sure. I peed, capped it, set it aside, washed my hands and walked out to the family room to straighten up a bit. A few minutes later, I walked back over to the bathroom and saw those two bright pink lines. Instantly I decided, "no, this is definitely the best day ever." I was pregnant. We were pregnant. I'm a mom.

It was early November, the time of year where everything is all warm and cozy, and everyone is reminded to count their blessings, and we were filled with gratitude. We waited until we were six weeks along to surprise our parents with little gift boxes that contained white bibs trimmed in orange with slices of pumpkin pie embroidered on them; the script read, "Grandma's Sweetie Pie." We arrived at each of their homes the morning of Thanksgiving and recorded their reactions – confusion, then clarity, surprise, joy, tears, and laughter.

Dark Clouds

Early in December, the spotting started. Just a trickle at first, and then growing heavier. I called the doctor, who sent us in for an early scan where we held hands as we looked up at a grayscale screen displaying a tiny little flicker of white. It was our baby's teeny heartbeat. They didn't tell us whether it was strong or not; no warning that this might be the start of a miscarriage. In fact, they didn't share much at all, just that our dates might be "off" by about a week or so and to go home and get some rest. The following week, I was on travel for a work conference that I'd spent the better part of the year planning, and it was finally time to execute. The conference was the capstone of my work at the time, and I was there on-site managing the event from early morning until early the next morning, resting just a few hours a night. When I saw the spotting again early morning in the hotel room, I instantly blamed myself. I wasn't resting enough, I was stressed, I had pushed myself too hard.

I called the doctor again. They did a scan like before. This time, an OB performed the scan. She prodded around and looked up at the screen. She was quiet, we were quiet, my husband and I held hands. "I'm sorry," her words broke the silence, and my breath was caught in my chest "there's no heartbeat." My husband nodded his head. "Okay," he said flatly. I sat silently.

The doctor continued, was still talking, spewing out all our "options." She was robotic almost as though she was rattling off a script, her words jumbled up and bumped into one together in my head, "a missed miscarriage... misoprostol... dilation and curettage... quite common... call our office to schedule the procedure... the next few days... risk of infection..." I stared silently.

She walked out of the examination room to "give us a minute." My husband held me tight as I sat on the examination table, the paper still draped over my bare legs, my arms hanging lifeless at my sides, his arms wrapped around them in spite of my not reciprocating his gesture. "It's going to be okay, babe." I nodded silently.

4

He handed me my clothes and helped me get dressed. Left leg, right leg. Left leg, right leg. We walked out of the examination room still hand in hand, continued out past the reception desk where the usually chipper trio of ladies out front looked my way knowingly and somberly. I walked past them silently, mustering a half smile, the left corner of my mouth turned upward just slightly. Together, we kept walking down the elevator, and out of the hospital's heavy mechanical doors. I walked silently.

The bitter cold winter air hit my face suddenly, and all at once, I broke my silence. Deep long sobs, indistinguishable words, hot, salty tears streamed from my eyes even as I squeezed them shut. Just a trickle at first, and then growing heavier.

The Wind Begins to Pickup

"It happens," they said. They shared stats, stories, and old wives' tales. A chorus of "just relax, it'll happen when it's supposed to" and "you know 'such and such' had a miscarriage and look at her kids now." We followed up with a new doctor, the Chief of Obstetrics & Gynecology for the hospital. He was kind and reassuring, "We don't know why this happened," he said "but sometimes it just does. What we do know is that there's a very small likelihood that this will happen again, less than 5%. You are both healthy, and the odds are in your favor. Give your body a cycle to recover, then feel free to try again." So we did.

By the first week of March, we were expecting again. We went in for a 7-and-a-half-week scan with the warm and kind doctor we'd meet with just before Christmas. He performed the scan himself and shared that he had seen a strong heartbeat. We talked to him about some upcoming travel, and he assured us it was "perfectly safe," we even joked about him coming with us! He asked us to come back in at 9 weeks to take another look before our trip. So we did.

"I'm so sorry," the technician started. I stared at the screen blurry-eyed. We were shocked, hell, even our doctor looked shocked. First at a visible loss for words, then apologizing repeatedly and genuinely. He promised we'd do more testing to get to the bottom of it. A blood work-up typically isn't recommended until you've had three losses, that's when you are classified as having had "recurrent miscarriage." But he signed off on the order right then, and several weeks later, we both drew blood. A week after that, I heard his voice on the other end of my phone. "Your husband's results all came back fine. The lab did, however, find a chromosomal translocation in your DNA that may point to the early losses. You are very healthy, and this doesn't affect your health, but it does make it challenging to have a baby."

And at that moment, I began to brace for the storm ahead. Two more pregnancies and two more losses later, the last of which was an ectopic pregnancy ending in one of my Fallopian tubes being removed; we were still without a living baby. What we did have through it all however,was a sense of peace. But it didn't begin that way.

Anchoring for the Storm

I was mad with God, and I told him so. Picture that. Little old me – one of the billions of humans to walk this planet (many of whom have faced far greater struggle) – mad with the Creator of the entire Universe. But I was, and you could tell me nothing.

Philippians 4:7 - "And the peace of God, which surpasses all understanding, will guard your hearts and your minds in Christ Jesus."

In time, however, after reading blogs and books, joining online support groups, and talking my husband's ear off about my feelings and frustrations, I realized that God was the only one who could truly make a difference. He is not only the author of my story, but the finisher of all things, and He was what I needed more than anything at that moment. He alone was my peace.

Romans 12:12 - "Be joyful in hope, patient in affliction, faithful in prayer."

Joyful in hope.

I believe in starting with gratitude. No matter what, there is always room for gratitude. Being grateful even in our loss, grief, and sorrow gives us even just a glimmer of hope. And, for me at least, hope was critical to changing my attitude from one of anger and frustration to one of joy and grace under fire.

Patient in affliction.

Gratitude comes naturally to me; patience doesn't. I'm talking about I don't have patience on a good day so exercising patience in a time of affliction was almost incomprehensible. For two and a half long, slow years, I suffered loss after loss in the one area I had been waiting my entire life for. And even now as I write these words and I continue to wait, I thank God that I'm building my patience muscles day by day because I have a feeling I will need a lot more of it, along with wisdom, and discernment the longer I live on this earth.

Faithful in prayer.

I began by talking to God, just talking. No fancy prayers, no specific petitions, just getting my feelings out. I talked to Him before bed and first thing in the morning, I talked to Him in the car, and out running errands, pretty soon God had drawn me so near to Him that I talked to Him all throughout the day and more than I talked to anyone else in my life, even those closest to me.

James 1:6 - But when you ask, you must believe and not doubt, because the one who doubts is like a wave of the sea, blown and tossed by the wind. (NIV)

The last couple of years have been a big time of transition for my husband and I. I left my career job of over 10 years, mere months after a major promotion that was a hefty boost to our family bottom line in favor of a $40,000 + pay cut to work in ministry full time. We then moved out of our townhome and into my parents' basement for 6 months as our first home was being built. Despite my strong feelings against this, I followed my husband's lead and God's urging toward obedience and humility. And in the same year, on what felt like an impulse, I decided to read the entire Bible cover to cover. This is something I never had an interest in doing before. I mean beyond "cherry picking" scriptural references and a few Bible study plans, I have never followed the story of the Bible chronologically, much less attempted to read the entire thing. But again, I was led, and I followed.

Unbeknownst to me as they were unfolding, these actions were not merely a coincidence; instead they were steps in God's divine strategy. Each of these acts of faith has proven to be huge assets as my husband and I sought out fertility treatment in the following year. Providing me with the flexibility at work, familial support and proximity, foundation in faith needed to carry me through an otherwise taxing and exhausting process. I was able to approach the process with belief and not doubt. I felt grounded and to anchored for the storm ahead so as not to be blown about and tossed by the wind, but instead to remain steadfast in the midst of it, even without knowledge of what lay ahead.

Psalms 55:8 - I would hurry to my shelter from the raging wind and the storm. (CSB)

While I don't know for certain which way the winds may blow, I know that God truly is my shelter in the storm. Regardless of the circumstance, the diagnosis, the fear of the unknown, or the feelings around what is known -- I'm ready. I am ready because I have found my peace and my safe space in the Lord, and through the provisions He has made available to me.

Reflection Questions:

- Write down 1-3 words you felt after reading this section.

- Rewrite a scripture that stood out the most. What did it mean to you?

- What is the one thing you can take from this story that will help move you along your journey while healing?

- List one thing you are grateful for while you prepare for the storm.

His Presence: In the Eye of the Storm

Part II by Alexis Harris Oluyole

Matthew 8:24 (NIV) - "Suddenly a furious storm came up on the lake, so that the waves swept over the boat. But Jesus was sleeping."

Ever felt like Jesus was silent or absent in the midst of a challenging situation in your life? I too know that feeling quite well! There is no worse feeling than feeling like you've been abandoned during a time when you needed God's help the most.

Torrential Downpour

"I'm having difficulty hearing a heartbeat," the nurse stated as she searched frantically for any signs of life found in my womb. I lay there calm, doing my best to exercise my mustard seed sized faith. I closed my eyes to bring myself ease as I waited for the doctor to enter the room. I saw my husband's face as I reflected back to that day the test finally read "pregnant." I could see his big pearly, white smile. Finally! We were so thrilled to be pregnant! It was certainly a struggle to get to this point, to say the least. Just a year earlier I had been recovering from surgery that would prepare us for this very moment. After months of intentional love-making in hopes of conceiving, like clock work, we were always greeted with disappointment of our failed attempts by my menstrual cycle that seemed to arrive without delay.

After consulting with my OB regarding this ongoing frustration, an MRI revealed what our next steps would have to be. To improve our ability to conceive, I would need to have several fibroids removed form my womb and one ovarian cyst- courtesy of a fancy medical procedure known as a laparoscopic myomectomy. The procedure would take approximately six weeks to recover from; likewise we were instructed that we would have to wait an additional nine plus months to begin trying to concieve. So you can imagine after patiently waiting for close to a year, when we saw that strip read pregnant, we felt that our family was finally coming together! I took multiple test just to be certain this was really happening! We held each other tightly, our eyes fixaed on the dark blue double lines piercing through the results window on all four tests. We stood there for a few moments basking in the excitement of what was to come. Finally, it's our turn!

I lay there as the doctor entered the room, wheeling in the sonogram machine. The squeaky wheel brought me back to the moment at hand. My anxiety began to heighten with each roll the probe made over my stomach. "I'm very concerned about what I'm seeing right now," he looked at me with great empathy. I lay there completely numb for a few minutes. This couldn't be right. This nurse, this doctor had to be playing some sinister prank. I was believing God for this. We were believing. My husband and I prayed for our baby; we planted our trust in the fact that God is able. How could this doctor be telling me my baby was no more? How could God do this to us? Yet, here we were face to face with this devastating news. Twenty-one weeks and his little life was gone just like that.

You'd think God would be done with me there, right? Wrong. Shortly after I found out my son was no more, the doctor hit me with another devastating blow. I would have to part with my uterus. That's right, you heard me, a partial hysterectomy. The ability to conceive on my own was no longer an option for my husband and I. Now, we are grieving two losses simultaneously. Just like that- my chances of becoming a mother, naturally, reduced dramatically. Throughout my pregnancy I had experienced ongoing light to moderate bleeding, and prior to becoming hospitalized, the doctors had me scheduled for a few test to determine the source of the bleeding. While I was admitted I got to complete all the exams needed for the team of specialist to make a determination. It was confirmed; along with placenta previa I had a condition called placenta accreta. This is a serious condition that occurs when the placenta grows too deeply into the uterine wall which can potentially cause great complications throughout pregnancy, including death upon delivery. The team of doctors tried their best to figure out a way to salvage my womb, but there ultimately was no way around it. In order for me to sustain my life, they would have to remove my uterus.

Once they delivered this news, from that point on everything else happened so quickly. The team of doctors had me scheduled for surgery early the next morning to remove my son and problematic uterus. However my body had other plans; it decided it could not hang on until the time resoluted by the physicians. It's like it just stopped fighting. Perhaps my feelings of grief and disappointment were just too great. Suddenly it had no reason to be strong anyore. My baby boy was ready to be relinquished from my weak womb, and he came through me on his own terms in a natural delivery around 3am on April 6, 2018. The doctors weren't prepared for him to do this, and quite frankly, neither was I.

The next thing I know, I'm being rushed to the operating room due to severe hemorrhaging. "This is it; I'm on my way out," I thought as the ceiling lights flashed by my eyes while they rushed me to the operating room. "First, my baby, and now me too, God? I thought you had more for our little family than this. Oh, well, at least I'll be with my son, he won't be alone." Then just like that, before the doctors could get the anesthesia prepared, my eyes closed.

Six intense hours and five units of blood later, I was being wheeled from the operating room to the IUC."Hey, baby, you made it,"my husband stated with a grateful tone, his eyes welled up with tears as he leaned over my bed in the ICU. I blinked my eyes, trying to refine my blurred vision. The surgeon walked into the room, and my husband ran to hug her while bursting into tears. "Thank you, thank you so much," I heard him say with great appreciation for her skilled hands, as I was still trying to come to life. She leaned over my bed angelic-like, and with a sweet, soft tone she said "You fought well. We have your baby waiting for you. Would you like to see him?" "NO!" I abruptly responded. At that moment, my heart could not bear the reality of viewing my lifeless child. "No, I don't want to see him," I continued. "Alright, I will have the nurse keep him for a day or so in case you change your mind."

I am forever grateful that the doctor requested that my son be retained and monitored by the nurses because, a few hours later, I did change my mind. I wanted to see and hold my boy. I held his lifeless little body in my arms, and in an instant, all the things I had hoped for him I could no longer see. Just like that, my little fighter had lost the fight. I let out a loud cry and wept in an inconsolable manner. I've never known such sorrow.

Violent Waves

Matthew 14:24 (MSG) - "Meanwhile, the boat was far out to sea when the wind came up against them and they were battered by the waves."

After losing my son, my thoughts and emotions began to spiral quickly. When I returned home from the hospital, everything felt so foreign. My home, my routine, my life. Just like that, I had to return to my day-to-day life. A life without him. How was I supposed to do that? You see, the day I found out he was growing inside me, my life changed at that very moment. The first time I heard his heartbeat, I knew my life would never be the same. I had created a little life. Now, I was forced to experience this new profound appreciation for that miracle of life without him? I found myself with more questions than answers. Feelings of anger, guilt, and betrayal began to flood my spirit and waves of confusion and doubt began to overtake me. I found myself set adrift, battered by my pain; questioning my beliefs.

Broken (adjective) - "violently separated into parts"

So I get to live, but he doesn't? Just like that, he's gone, and I don't understand why. Did I not pray enough? Was my faith lacking? Did I offend you, God?! Why my baby? Why me? Sure, I'm not perfect, but don't you see these other jokers who behave far worse? Don't they get to be parents? Don't they get to experience motherhood? It's not fair.

Sometimes in those unbearable moments, when life has taken you in an unexpected painful direction, and you don't know what to say, Jesus is there saying it all for you. Sometimes the pain or the grief of what we are dealing with is so much; it drains life from our spirit and makes us question everything. I thank God for The Intercessor.

Romans 8:25-27 - "But if we hope for what we do not yet have, we wait for it patiently. In the same way, the Spirit helps us in our weakness. We do not know what we ought to pray for, but the spirit himself intercedes for us with groans that words cannot express. And he who searches our hearts knows the mind of the Spirit, because the spirit intercedes for the saints in accordance with God's will." (NIV)

I didn't know what to think, let alone pray. At this point, I was convinced that I had fallen off of God's radar entirely. I was numb. My heart was broken. There will come a time in your life when you will be filled with so many emotions you will not know how to process any of them. In those moments, you will just have to 'be' and allow Jesus to intercede for the pain, the frustration, the anxiety, or whatever it is you are feeling. With so many emotions racing inside of me, I did not know what to pray. All I could do was cry out "Why Lord? Why?"

Guilt (noun) - "a feeling of deserving blame for offenses"

Tell me, Father, what did I do? I had to do something terrible to offend you for this to be my outcome. I know what it was. I enjoyed my single life a bit too much, didn't I? I didn't keep myself pure. I entertained the empty relationships. I didn't follow your direction or patiently wait for you. I indulged, I did me. That has to be it. Maybe it's because I didn't believe enough? I know what it was, I was too busy. I put my career first. I didn't trust that you would provide for our family if I scaled things back some. Maybe we should confront the elephant in the room; was it because I married a man who is divorced? We know that divorce is frowned upon. Certainly, you must be punishing us both for this. This is what some of our peers would have us to believe, so it must be some truth to it. I'm sorry we offended you, God. Our innocent baby didn't have to pay the price.

Anger (noun) - "a strong feeling of annoyance, displeasure, or hostility."

So many unanswered questions. How could you not let him experience our love? Why did you rob me of his love? Why this way? So many unanswered questions. I don't know what to say. I don't know what to think. I have no idea what to pray. I feel like I have no idea who you are. You overlooked me. You disappointed me, yet you call me your child, your daughter? This isn't fair. It hurts. My precious baby, my wounded womb, you have left me with nothing but physical and emotional pain.

"You're so strong." "Your faith is admirable." I don't want to hear this sh*t! I'm tired of being "the strong one." How has my strength served me? Hmm, let's see. Can I feel my strength growing inside of me? Can I hold and kiss my strength? All this strength seems to do is qualify me for more challenges, and if it's between being strong or being a mother, I'd rather have my son, please. I want my child like the rest of these folks who you've deemed worthy to be parents. What makes them so different from me? "

16

God gives the toughest battles to his strongest warriors." I hate clichés! Keep that! I want my promise!How often do we hear these comments that are aimed to offer support, but mostly feel like a dagger to the heart? People try their best to encourage us when we are going through hurtful experiences, but honestly, it's not easy trying to figure out the right things to say. That's because there is no right thing to say. When someone suffers a devastating loss, disappointment, illness, etc., there are no words that ease the pain, frustration, and anger. So here's a tip, if you don't know what to say, say just that. No need to try to improvise. No need to try and place the band-aid of a few scriptures on a massive wound.

The one thing that truly bothers me about many church services nowadays is that no one wants to address the difficult conversations! Not many preachers prepare you for when God flat out says, "no"! Instead, we are encouraged over and over to exercise our "mustard seed" of faith, no matter how the outcome may be presenting. We don't hear much teaching around fellowship in faith through suffering. Yet the reality is, suffering is a very relevant part of our development as believers.

I'm not going to church. A 'feel good' message can't help me get through this. I need a break from it all, you too, God.

Incomplete (adjective) - *"not having all the necessary or appropriate parts"*

Six long grueling months, my patient, loving husband went without the "wet, wet" (one of our affectionate terms for sex). It wasn't easy by any means, managing my mood swings and cravings, yet receiving minimal to no physical output on my end. My pregnancy was a very high risk, so "no sex" was echoed to us at every wellness checkup. My poor baby was beyond sexually frustrated, but he held strong. So you can imagine how pumped we both were that I was all healed up from surgery. Sure, it was taking some time for my emotional healing to catch up with my physical recovery, but that was to be expected. We were both ready for some tender loving!

Finally, the moment was here, and we could both feel the depths of our love as we held each other close, enjoying one another. My body was still trying to figure itself out from the removal of my womb. Somewhat tender, I felt more pain than pleasure. We held each other close, determined to reclaim our sexual energy. Then the moment we both enjoyed pre-surgery (the climax) had arrived. Yet post-surgery, it felt much different. Instead of riding a high, we were greeted with a sense of hollowness. Just like that, we were both reminded that our love no longer held the ability to reproduce on its own. What a somber reality. My husband held me as I wept. "Father, are you there?" my spirit whispered. "Help me; help me, please."

Calming Waters

Psalms 107:29 (NIV) - "He stilled the storm to a whisper; the waves of the sea were hushed."

Reconcile (verb) - "Restore friendly relations between"

God had allowed my world to be shaken upside down and turned inside out. I was still aching. I couldn't focus. I felt stuck. Why weren't things moving in the right direction in my life? Why did everything have to be a struggle? My husband and I had stagnation in our careers, we had lost opportunities, and were barely hanging on to some friendships. Now, our precious child. I felt like a failure. I felt unsuccessful. Then God began to reveal some things to me in the midst of my hurting. He said to me that *success is the manifestation of your destiny.*

Our destiny is most often birthed out through our pain and suffering, the intimate moments between God and us, where we have labored and travailed with Him as we have waited for the next step or level to arrive. Just as a woman undergoes physical labor pains before giving birth to her child, we also suffer spiritual labor of our own. We have pain, we have discomfort, our minds and bodies stretched beyond what we feel are our limits; then finally, when we least expect it, purpose is found, clarity is reached, and our destiny is birthed!

Before Jesus encountered His destiny, He had to endure great pain, even before He hung on the cross. With each new phase He encountered before Calvary, He prayed and communed with God. With all the miracles Jesus performed, none of them mattered at that moment. He did not pray and remind God of all the wonderful things He had done. Jesus prayed for strength and courage so that God's will would prevail (John 17: 1-5; Matthew 26: 38-39 NIV). Jesus understood that His destiny was to be birthed through His suffering. We, as followers of Christ, often forget that we too have to fellowship with Him through joy and suffering.

1 Peter 2:19-21 (NIV) - "For it is commendable if a man bears up under the pain of unjust suffering because he is conscious of God. But how is it to your credit if you receive a beating for doing wrong and endure it? But if you suffer for doing good and you endure it, this is commendable before God. To this you were called, because Christ suffered for you, leaving you an example that you should follow in his steps."

It is the agony of the suffering that is designed to bring us closer to God, and it is as we move closer to Him, that we experience peace. When we are in a peaceful state, then God can move, and His glory can be revealed. Yet, as soon as we are faced with adversity and pain, we immediately panic or become angry. We immediately blame God. We remind Him of all the sacrifices we have made and all the wonderful works we have done, instead of seeking His guidance and trusting His ability to keep us anchored through it all. Nobody likes pain, yet some situations in life will be tough and perhaps even hurtful. We must trust in God and allow Him to guide us through the painful moments in our lives. The painful moments will help to establish our future success.

Healing (noun) - "the process of making or becoming sound or healthy again."

Here I am, face-to-face with my faith. I have some tough choices to make. Do I continue to believe, although a part of me feels failed as a Christian and as His daughter? Can I push past how I feel? Do I make a choice to rely on what I know? To survive this pain and devastation, it may be in my best interest to focus on what I've learned thus far as His daughter. If this becomes my choice, then here is the hard truth before me: *there is no salvation apart from suffering.*

Could He have allowed this to play out differently? Absolutely. Why didn't He?! I may never fully know this until I'm face to face with Him. What I do know is the word He has left to keep me focused on the fact that He is with me, which is:

Isaiah 41:10 (NIV) - "Do not fear, for I am with you; do not be dismayed, for I am your God. I will strengthen you and help you; I will uphold you with my righteous right hand."

Isaiah 55:8-9 (NLT) - "My thoughts are nothing like your thoughts," says the Lord. "And my ways are far beyond anything you could imagine"

1 Peter 5:8-10 (NIV) - "Be alert and of sober mind. Your enemy the devil prowls around like a roaring lion looking for someone to devour. Resist him, standing firm in the faith, because you know that the family of believers throughout the world is undergoing the same kind of sufferings. And the God of all grace, who called you to his eternal glory in Christ, after you have suffered a little while, will himself restore you and make you strong, firm and steadfast."

Philippians 4: 6-7 (NIV) - "Do not be anxious about anything, but in every situation, by prayer and petition, with thanksgiving, present your requests to God. And the peace of God, which transcends all understanding, will guard your hearts and your minds in Christ Jesus."

Romans 5:1-5 (NKJV) - "Therefore, having been justified by faith, we have a peace with God through our Lord Jesus Christ...And not only that, but we also glory in tribulations, knowing that tribulation produces perseverance; and perseverance, character; and character, hope. Now hope does not disappoint."

These scriptures continue to serve as a source of affirmation that although the storm has left me in ruins, a time of recoupment is coming. I could continue to question; I have every right to be bitter and angry. Trust me, these emotions try to surface. They are very real and raw; profound and prevalent. However, again, I have some serious choices to make. Do I want to be angry or justified? Do I want to be bitter or justified? Do I want to feel incomplete or do I want to be made whole having been justified by faith? Not because I believed and received, but because I believed, and still believe, even though I did not.

The fact of the matter is that God never promised that His answers to our request or petitions would always be: yes. He did say, however, that His peace would "transcend all understanding." He said that His "grace is sufficient" (2 Corinthians 12:9 NKJV). Every day, I'm captivated by his grace as I follow His direction. Each day, I feel the peace that only He can provide as I seek Him in prayer. The storm is passing now, and I can feel sunlight on my face. A rainbow is coming.

Reflection Questions:

- Write down 1-3 words you felt after reading this section:

- Rewrite a scripture that stood out the most. What did it mean to you?

- What is the one thing you can take from this story that will help move you along your journey while healing?

- List one thing you are grateful for while in the midst of your storm:

His Power: Rainbows and Reflections

Part III by Sedria Wilson

Where to even begin. As I think about my life and all its trials and struggles, all I can say at the end of all of it is, "Thank you, Jesus, for never leaving my side and keeping me grounded during those trying times." I truly believe that I would have lost my entire mind if it wasn't for his strength, mercy, and grace as my faith was tested in more ways than one. I truly know now that when I was created, God made me extra special to endure a lot of unfortunate pain.

Genesis 9:15-16 - "Never again will the waters become a flood to destroy all life. Whenever the rainbow appears in the clouds, I will see it and remember the everlasting covenant between God and all living creatures of every kind on the earth."

It is due to this scripture that rainbows have so much more meaning to my life now. At first, I always felt myself connected to butterflies because they represent freedom, and the amazing change that one can have from within. Rainbows, however, are one of God's most stunning creations. To see the various colors come together to create something so beautiful is absolutely amazing, as color variations are the perfect way to describe my emotions during a very dark time in my life.

Bright, Yellow Sunshine

As I was fully engrossed in the final stages of planning my wedding, a week before the big day, I found out I was pregnant. "OMG!!!! This is absolutely amazing", and all I could think about now was being well on my way to start expanding my new little family. This is something I have always dreamed about as a little girl. I was finally getting my wish. However, while being excited, I was scared as well. I just didn't know what to expect. My best friend went with me to the doctor to confirm everything was all good with the baby. This was my first pregnancy, so I just needed to be sure. My husband and I were going to Paris and London for our honeymoon, so I remember asking the doctor if it was okay for me to fly. The doctor laughed and said at this stage in my pregnancy, I can do a lot of things, and one of them is flying. My only orders were to get married, have fun, and avoid as much secondhand smoke in Europe as possible.

As my pregnancy progressed, I remained in a very happy state. Looking at baby items, thinking about names, wondering if baby was a boy or a girl. Then as a little time progressed, I heard the doctor say "Congratulations, you're having a boy!" I could not have been any happier. My husband just knew we were having a boy, so once it was confirmed, it was time to celebrate.

Bittersweet and Somber Blue

In March of 2012, I began to have some pain in my abdomen that would go on and off. This was the type of pain I had never felt before. When the pain did not subside on its own, I decided to go to the doctor to have them see if anything was going on with the baby. The nurse practitioner performed an ultrasound of my belly, felt my cervix and then said some dreadful words that I will never forget, "Honey, right now, you are in preterm labor, and we have to admit you right away to see if we can stop the contractions." Talk about being scared and confused all at the same time. I was only 23 weeks at this time, how could I be in labor? I am young, healthy, and this is my first pregnancy. The doctors tried everything that they could to stop the contractions, but I was too far along. Shortly after the confirmation that I was going to be delivering our baby very soon, multiple doctors came into the hospital room to speak with my husband and me about our "options."

What do you mean "options?" In my mind, my only option was to deliver my son and take him home. But the doctors knew this would not be the case. I did not understand what was happening. We were being asked questions like, "Do you want us to perform CPR if he doesn't come out viable?" "Would you like for us to call in the hospital Chaplain for prayer?" Oh my goodness, I had never felt an emotional pain like this in my life. Even after losing both of my parents, this was a different type of pain. I was so worried about my baby. My first born.

I just cried, cried, and cried some more.

Philippians 4:13 - "I can do everything through Christ that gives me strength."

This passage played over and over in my head during this process. I knew my son was coming, and with no epidural, as his mother, I knew it was my duty to fight for him even in the midst of him feeling weak.

After just a few hours of labor, we welcomed into the world our beautiful baby boy, Taylor Jeremiah Wilson, weighing in a little over one pound on March 13, 2012. He came out crying, making soft, subtle noises. That was a good sign! The doctors then immediately took him to the NICU, and this was the start of our four-month hospital journey for his care, which began to seem like a lifetime. I was exhausted and on edge a lot. Every time my phone rang when I was not at the hospital, it just made me so sick. I just didn't know what news I was going to get. I tried to jump back into my everyday routine, working full time, newlywed wife, and step-mom also known as "MiMi" to my amazing oldest bonus son. I was pumping breast milk at work then leaving so I can take it to the hospital so they could feed it to him through his feeding tube. As his mother, I tried and did everything possible that I could think of for my boy, so that he knew that he was loved.

My sweet baby was a true fighter. I could begin to see the look on the doctor's faces as time went on that he would not survive this fight. He was just born too early.

Seeing Red

Beep... Beep... Beep... Beep... Beep. That was the sound that I heard constantly while living in the NICU for about four months. Monitors were constantly going off around me. If not for my own child, then for someone else's. Seeing and hearing doctors and nurses making their rounds, going room by room, discussing the medical plan of action for each patient that day. The smell of sick children constantly being cared for is something I will never forget. Seeing the look of pity on some of the nurse's faces when they enter your room to begin caring for your baby. Looking at your child being fed through tubes, watching him get agitated when getting pricked for blood to be drawn, crying when in pain, and too fragile to hold; the emotional scars from all of this cut deep into my soul.

Having to wash my hands and arms for an extensive period of time with a special soap to keep the germs down. The emotional roller coaster of my child having good days and bad days. Praying so hard on my knees for God to heal my child and for surgeries to go well. After multiple treatments and tests, hospital transfers, surgeries, and discussions about his next plan of care, my dear son left us on earth to be with the Lord and become our forever angel on July 19, 2012. The same month he was supposed to be born if I had him full term. I cried, cried, cried, and cried even more than I thought I could.

My child is gone. All of this, and my child is gone.

I was extremely sad, upset, frustrated, confused, lonely, and heartbroken. I felt cheated of what was part of my happily ever after. We did all that we could to ensure things were getting done and going in the right direction. I was pissed!!!! Nobody prepared us for this to happen. But then again, how could they?

My struggle and anger towards God have now begun. God, how could you? Really? Why me? I don't understand why you would take my first born away from me. After all I have already gone through, you cannot be serious. These were all thoughts that I battled with in my head. There was nothing that anyone could say to me to help me feel better. I was mad as hell inside. However, I kept finding myself trying to be strong for others, but yet I was the one suffering. Our marriage was being tested already in the first 7 months. Seeing that my husband and I grieve so differently was a true struggle. I began to withdraw myself and internalize a lot in my head. It was not a good space to be in at all. I did not want to engage in sex, and my emotional connectedness was greatly affected. It was not a good space to be in at all.

Joshua 1:9 - "Be bold. Be brave. Be courageous."

I felt so alone. I just knew I was the only one going through this. This type of thing does not happen to women anymore, let alone me. What did I do to deserve this? To see my family and friends around me grieve and mourn the death of my son was so painful to watch. I began to not like myself and my body, and it showed up big time, in my marriage. I kept so much emotion inside to the point that seeking counseling was a must. There was no way I could continue like this, and I was not about to let this continue to break my spirit. That's when I sought out the Bible for encouragement. The scripture that I kept near to my heart and mind when I began feeling discouraged and defeated was:

Psalms 37:5 - "Commit your way to the Lord. Trust in Him, and He will act."

Now let's talk about defeat. Defeat. Defeat. Defeat. I just knew I was going to lose this battle. I struggled with the fact that I felt like I failed my husband. How could I do this to him? Am I not going to be able to give him another child? He chose me as his wife, and I immediately caused him so much pain. Well, at least that is how I felt. He would tell me over and over again that it was going to be okay, and he never blamed me for anything. In fact, he was very encouraging and strong the entire time, but I just could not help but feel this way despite his words and actions. Seeing his love for his first son was such a sight to see. This is one of the many reasons why I love this man. This is why I wanted to give him another child, one whom he really wanted. I would look at my bonus son and ask God to give me the strength to continue to love. My heart and love for him grew so much more. To this day, everyone knows that boy is my life, and I am so thankful for him. He was only 5 years old when his brother passed away, so we knew as his parents we needed to be there for him as well.

A Tiny Green Sprout: Growing Something New

October 31, 2012, I found out I was pregnant. I am pregnant. I am pregnant? Damn. Not yet. How did this happen? Well, I know how this happened, but I was beyond scared because we did not plan to try again so soon! I had a plan in place with my doctors to have my fibroids removed, have more conversations around explaining why I went into preterm labor, and setting an action plan for the next time we'd conceive. But God had His own plan.

The doctors diagnosed me with an incompetent cervix. What does that mean? Simply put, it is when the cervix begins to open early, causing one to go into preterm labor. When I found out I was pregnant for the second time, I was not happy at all. I had a range of emotions that I could not shake off. I told my husband that I was not ready. I was scared that the same thing would happen again.

I had to endure a surgical procedure to insert a cerclage to help keep my cervix closed, weekly progesterone shots to help maintain those hormone levels, and did I mention no sex? Yup, you heard right. No sex for my entire pregnancy. It was a lot. Then to add the icing on the cake, I found out the sex of the baby. A baby GIRL. My husband is the oldest of five boys, so having a little girl has always been a wish. So yes, the pressure was on a sistah's shoulders, heavy.

I was definitely stressed and scared to death. Every move I made, I was trying to see how I felt. Constantly waiting for the baby to kick. Always monitoring any pain that I had. My stress level was at an all-time high. Family members had to constantly tell me to calm down and not to worry. But that was so hard for me. How could I not worry? All I knew was that I did not want what happened with Taylor to happen again. I would not have been able to handle that at all. When I reached 23 weeks, I felt so relieved, and every week after was progress in my mind. I knew that my baby girl would have more of a chance of survival at that point, and she did! During the first half of my pregnancy, there was so much worry, but God showed me an immediate sign that everything was going to work out. I knew I coud do this. God led me through this process, and He kept me and my family safe.

Romans 8:18 - "The pain that you've been feeling, can't compare to the joy that's coming."

On July 2, 2013, God blessed me and my family with a healthy, beautiful baby girl. She literally took my breath away. I could not believe I was holding my daughter, whom I thought I would never have. I viewed the world so differently at this moment. God showed up for me. God showed up for my family. God showed us that if you just believe and have faith, He will deliver on His promise.

Purple Clouds of Peace and Contentment

"So when are you having the next one? You guys don't want just one more?" These are the types of questions my husband and I get asked all the time. I get it, I really do, but no, thank you.

When I look up in the evening sky, purple clouds are what I see. There is so much beauty and mystery in the sky. Sometimes, I can just get lost in my thoughts while looking at the sky and reflecting. The color purple can represent so many different things, but for me, it represents: peace, grace, devotion, royalty, and wisdom. For as long as I can remember, I have always been drawn to the color purple, and now I fully understand why. Things don't come around full circle for no reason. God's hand and His plan have always been in the mix.

I am thankful for God's unwavering hands. God has opened up this door for me to share my story and be a beacon of light to other women who are going through or have gone through this type of pain.

It is my hope that a poem that I wrote to myself a few years ago for encouragement yields the same outcome for others:

Never lose sight of what is most important.

Never give up.

Don't let the petty things get in your way and block your blessings.

Continue to glow up and stay fabulous. People are always watching you.

Be the example. Be God's example.

As I continue to write my story, I am proud to say that our family is complete. Today, my husband and I have an 11-year-old growing intelligent and funny man-child, a 5-year old feisty, smart, and independent daughter, and the best guardian angel in Heaven, Taylor. To this day, our son is still a major part of our lives. His birthday and the day of his passing are always celebrated and honored. I will continue to support women and organizations that work hard to help bring awareness to premature births, birth defects, and infant mortality.

Proverbs 13:12 - "Hope deferred makes the heart sick, but when the desire is fulfilled, it is a tree of life."

#NoFurtherExplainationNeeded #GodsPlan

Reflection Questions:

- Write down 1-3 words you felt after reading this section:

- Rewrite a scripture that stood out the most. What did it mean to you?

- What is the one thing you can take from this story that will help move you along your journey while healing?

- List one thing you are grateful for while reflecting on God's grace as the storm has passed:

Epilogue

Power In The Pain

Romans 5:1 (NKJV) - "Therefore, having been justified by faith, we have a peace with God..."

We hope that reading our various stories has helped to keep you encouraged and move you along to a place of hope for with whatever challenge you may be facing. It is our prayer that you view your circumstance, whether past or present, as an experience that has positioned you for power. That's right power- girl power! There is power in overcoming loss and hardships. God is forging something beautiful in your life, but it can only be unleashed through trust and resiliency. He is waiting to reveal His glory if you will allow yourself to be completely "justified by faith!" This means embracing all that you have suffered as part of a more carefully guided event that will move you forward in life beyond anything you ever imagined.

This means understanding that, although you may feel alone, you are not alone. We are with you. God is with you; always preserving and pursuing you even when you feel that life is hurting you.

Psalms 46:1 (NLT) - "God is our refuge and strength, always ready to help in times of trouble."

When you allow yourself to view challenging circumstance from this lens, you will position yourself for power because you are no longer restricted by your feelings of pain or disappointment. Pray and ask for help daily that He guides you to a place of reliance in Him, even when you don't understand how the path is unfolding. God can then reveal things to you that will bring you peace and recoup your joy.

Know that you are a part of a sisterhood of believers who understand you and have suffered with you. The Bible speaks of us bearing each other's burdens as one body:

Galatians 6: 2 (NIV) -Carry each other's burdens, and in this way you will fulfill the law of Christ.

1 Corinthians 12:24-26 (NIV) - God has put the body together, giving greater honor to the parts that lacked it, so that there should be no division in the body, but that its parts should have equal concern for each other. If one part suffers, every part suffers with it; if one part is honored, every part rejoices with it.

Together, we will overcome every challenge that the enemy would attempt to use to keep us entangled in disbelief. Together, we dispel any feelings of worry or anxiety regarding God's plan for the progression of our life. We as sisters in Christ by the support of the holy spirit approach each day with a sense of peace that surpasses all logic and understanding in the name of Jesus! May God keep you always!

Numbers 6:24-26 (NLT) - "May the Lord bless you and protect you. May the Lord smile on you and be gracious to you. May the Lord show his favor toward you, and give you his peace."

Women of the Bible Who Endured Fertility Challenges

Sarah and Abraham:

Sarai, Abram's wife, hadn't yet produced a child. She had an Egyptian maid named Hagar. Sarai said to Abram, "God has not seen fit to let me have a child. Sleep with my maid. Maybe I can get a family from her." Abram agreed to do what Sarai said (Genesis 16:1-2 MSG).

"Hagar gave Abram a son. Abram named him Ishmael. Abram was eighty-six years old when Hagar gave him his son, Ishmael" (Genesis 16:15-16 MSG).

When Abram was ninety-nine years old, God showed up and said to him, "I am The Strong God, live entirely before me, live to the hilt! I'll make a covenant between us and I'll give you a huge family." (Genesis 17:1-2 MSG)

God continued speaking to Abraham, "And Sarai your wife: Don't call her Sarai any longer; call her Sarah. I'll bless her—yes! I'll give you a son by her! Oh, how I'll bless her! Nations will come from her; kings of nations will come from her."

Abraham fell flat on his face. And then he laughed, thinking, "Can a hundred-year-old man father a son? And can Sarah, at ninety years, have a baby?"

Recovering, Abraham said to God, "Oh, keep Ishmael alive and well before you!"

But God said, "That's not what I mean. Your wife, Sarah, will have a baby, a son. Name him Isaac (Laughter). I'll establish my covenant with him and his descendants, a covenant that lasts forever (Genesis 17:15-19 MSG).

Now the Lord was gracious to Sarah as he had said, and the Lord did for Sarah what he had promised. Sarah became pregnant and bore a son to Abraham in his old age, at the very time God had promised him. Abraham gave the name Isaac to the son Sarah bore him.4 When his son Isaac was eight days old, Abraham circumcised him, as God commanded him. Abraham was a hundred years old when his son Isaac was born to him.

Sarah said, "God has brought me laughter, and everyone who hears about this will laugh with me." And she added, "Who would have said to Abraham that Sarah would nurse children? Yet I have borne him a son in his old age (Genesis 21:15-19 MSG)."

Both Abraham and Sarah continued to grow older in age. Before his death Abraham seeks out a wife for his son Isaac. Read Genesis 24.

Isaac and Rebekah:

This is the family tree of Isaac son of Abraham: Abraham had Isaac. Isaac was forty years old when he married Rebekah daughter of Bethuel the Aramean of Paddan Aram. She was the sister of Laban the Aramean.

Isaac prayed hard to God for his wife because she was barren. God answered his prayer and Rebekah became pregnant. But the children tumbled and kicked inside her so much that she said, "If this is the way it's going to be, why go on living?" She went to God to find out what was going on. God told her,

Two nations are in your womb,

two peoples butting heads while still in your body.

One people will overpower the other,

and the older will serve the younger."

When her time to give birth came, sure enough, there were twins in her womb. The first came out reddish, as if snugly wrapped in a hairy blanket; they named him Esau (Hairy). His brother followed, his fist clenched tight to Esau's heel; they named him Jacob (Heel).

Isaac was sixty years old when they were born (Genesis 25:19-26 MSG)." Rebekah and Isaac had their children after 20 years.

Jacob and his brother grow older with rivalry between them. Isaac orders Jacob to leave home and take up a wife after he receives his brother Esau's blessing under false pretenses (Genesis 27-29).

Rachel and Jacob:

Now Laban had two daughters; Leah was the older and Rachel the younger. Leah had nice eyes, but Rachel was stunningly beautiful. And it was Rachel that Jacob loved.

So Jacob answered, "I will work for you seven years for your younger daughter Rachel."

"It is far better," said Laban, "that I give her to you than marry her to some outsider. Yes. Stay here with me."

So Jacob worked seven years for Rachel. But it only seemed like a few days, he loved her so much.

Then Jacob said to Laban, "Give me my wife; I've completed what we agreed I'd do. I'm ready to consummate my marriage." Laban invited everyone around and threw a big feast. At evening, though, he got his daughter Leah and brought her to the marriage bed, and Jacob slept with her. (Laban gave his maid Zilpah to his daughter Leah as her maid.)

Morning came: There was Leah in the marriage bed!

Jacob confronted Laban, "What have you done to me? Didn't I work all this time for the hand of Rachel? Why did you cheat me?"

"We don't do it that way in our country," said Laban. "We don't marry off the younger daughter before the older. Enjoy your week of honeymoon, and then we'll give you the other one also. But it will cost you another seven years of work."

Jacob agreed. When he'd completed the honeymoon week, Laban gave him his daughter Rachel to be his wife. (Laban gave his maid Bilhah to his daughter Rachel as her maid.) Jacob then slept with her. And he loved Rachel more than Leah. He worked for Laban another seven years.

When God realized that Leah was unloved, he opened her womb. But Rachel was barren. Leah became pregnant and had a son. She named him Reuben (Look-It's-a-Boy!). "This is a sign," she said, "that God has seen my misery; and a sign that now my husband will love me."

She became pregnant again and had another son. "God heard," she said, "that I was unloved and so he gave me this son also." She named this one Simeon (God-Heard). She became pregnant yet again—another son. She said, "Now maybe my husband will connect with me—I've given him three sons!" That's why she named him Levi (Connect). She became pregnant a final time and had a fourth son. She said, "This time I'll praise God." So she named him Judah (Praise-God). Then she stopped having children (Genesis 29:16-35 MSG).

When Rachel realized that she wasn't having any children for Jacob, she became jealous of her sister. She told Jacob, "Give me sons or I'll die!"

Jacob got angry with Rachel and said, "Am I God? Am I the one who refused you babies?"

Rachel said, "Here's my maid Bilhah. Sleep with her. Let her substitute for me so I can have a child through her and build a family." So she gave him her maid Bilhah for a wife and Jacob slept with her. Bilhah became pregnant and gave Jacob a son.

Rachel said, "God took my side and vindicated me. He listened to me and gave me a son." She named him Dan (Vindication). Rachel's maid Bilhah became pregnant again and gave Jacob a second son. Rachel said, "I've been in an all-out fight with my sister—and I've won." So she named him Naphtali (Fight).

When Leah saw that she wasn't having any more children, she gave her maid Zilpah to Jacob for a wife. Zilpah had a son for Jacob. Leah said, "How fortunate!" and she named him Gad (Lucky). When Leah's maid Zilpah had a second son for Jacob, Leah said, "A happy day! The women will congratulate me in my happiness." So she named him Asher (Happy) (Genesis 30: 1-13 MSG).

"When Jacob came home that evening from the fields, Leah was there to meet him: "Sleep with me tonight; I've bartered my son's mandrakes for a night with you." So he slept with her that night. God listened to Leah; she became pregnant and gave Jacob a fifth son. She said, "God rewarded me for giving my maid to my husband." She named him Issachar (Bartered). Leah became pregnant yet again and gave Jacob a sixth son, saying, "God has given me a great gift. This time my husband will honor me with gifts—I've given him six sons!" She named him Zebulun (Honor). Last of all she had a daughter and named her Dinah.

And then God remembered Rachel. God listened to her and opened her womb. She became pregnant and had a son. She said, "God has taken away my humiliation." She named him Joseph (Add), praying, "May God add yet another son to me" (Genesis 30: 16-24 MSG).

God did eventually allow Rachel to conceive and she gave birth to another son, Benjamin (Genesis 35: 16-18 MSG).

The Wife of Manoah:

Although the scriptures do not name her, they do tell us that, Manoah, from the tribe of Dan, was married to a wife who couldn't bear him any children.

And then the People of Israel were back at it again, doing what was evil in God's sight. God put them under the domination of the Philistines for forty years.

At that time there was a man named Manoah from Zorah from the tribe of Dan. His wife was barren and childless. The angel of God appeared to her and told her, "I know that you are barren and childless, but you're going to become pregnant and bear a son. But take much care: Drink no wine or beer; eat nothing ritually unclean. You are, in fact, pregnant right now, carrying a son. No razor will touch his head—the boy will be God's Nazirite from the moment of his birth. He will launch the deliverance from Philistine oppression."

The woman went to her husband and said, "A man of God came to me. He looked like the angel of God—terror laced with glory! I didn't ask him where he was from and he didn't tell me his name, but he told me, 'You're pregnant. You're going to give birth to a son. Don't drink any wine or beer and eat nothing ritually unclean. The boy will be God's Nazirite from the moment of birth to the day of his death.'"

Manoah prayed to God: "Master, let the man of God you sent come to us again and teach us how to raise this boy who is to be born."

God listened to Manoah. God's angel came again to the woman. She was sitting in the field; her husband Manoah wasn't there with her. She jumped to her feet and ran and told her husband: "He's back! The man who came to me that day!"

Manoah got up and, following his wife, came to the man. He said to him, "Are you the man who spoke to my wife?"

He said, "I am."

Manoah said, "So. When what you say comes true, what do you have to tell us about this boy and his work?"

The angel of God said to Manoah, "Keep in mind everything I told the woman. Eat nothing that comes from the vine: Drink no wine or beer; eat no ritually unclean foods. She's to observe everything I commanded her."

Manoah said to the angel of God, "Please, stay with us a little longer; we'll prepare a meal for you—a young goat."

God's angel said to Manoah, "Even if I stay, I won't eat your food. But if you want to prepare a Whole-Burnt-Offering for God, go ahead—offer it!" Manoah had no idea that he was talking to the angel of God.

Then Manoah asked the angel of God, "What's your name? When your words come true, we'd like to honor you."

The angel of God said, "What's this? You ask for my name? You wouldn't understand—it's sheer wonder."

"So Manoah took the kid and the Grain-Offering and sacrificed them on a rock altar to God who works wonders. As the flames leapt up from the altar to heaven, God's angel also ascended in the altar flames. When Manoah and his wife saw this, they fell facedown to the ground. Manoah and his wife never saw the angel of God again."

Only then did Manoah realize that this was God's angel. He said to his wife, "We're as good as dead! We've looked on God!"

"But his wife said, "If God were planning to kill us, he wouldn't have accepted our Whole-Burnt-Offering and Grain-Offering, or revealed all these things to us—given us this birth announcement."

"The woman gave birth to a son. They named him Samson. The boy grew and God blessed him. The Spirit of God began working in him while he was staying at a Danite camp between Zorah and Eshtaol" (Judges 13:1-25 MSG).

Hannah and Elkanah:

There was a certain man from Ramathaim, a Zuphite from the hill country of Ephraim, whose name was Elkanah son of Jeroham, the son of Elihu, the son of Tohu, the son of Zuph, an Ephraimite. He had two wives; one was called Hannah and the other Peninnah. Peninnah had children, but Hannah had none."

Year after year this man went up from his town to worship and sacrifice to the Lord Almighty at Shiloh, where Hophni and Phinehas, the two sons of Eli, were priests of the Lord. Whenever the day came for Elkanah to sacrifice, he would give portions of the meat to his wife Peninnah and to all her sons and daughters. But to Hannah he gave a double portion because he loved her, and the Lord had closed her womb. Because the Lord had closed Hannah's womb, her rival kept provoking her in order to irritate her. This went on year after year. Whenever Hannah went up to the house of the Lord, her rival provoked her till she wept and would not eat. Her husband Elkanah would say to her, "Hannah, why are you weeping? Why don't you eat? Why are you downhearted? Don't I mean more to you than ten sons?"

Once when they had finished eating and drinking in Shiloh, Hannah stood up. Now Eli the priest was sitting on his chair by the doorpost of the Lord's house. In her deep anguish Hannah prayed to the Lord, weeping bitterly. And she made a vow, saying, "Lord Almighty, if you will only look on your servant's misery and remember me, and not forget your servant but give her a son, then I will give him to the Lord for all the days of his life, and no razor will ever be used on his head."

As she kept on praying to the Lord, Eli observed her mouth. Hannah was praying in her heart, and her lips were moving but her voice was not heard. Eli thought she was drunk and said to her, "How long are you going to stay drunk? Put away your wine."

"Not so, my lord," Hannah replied, "I am a woman who is deeply troubled. I have not been drinking wine or beer; I was pouring out my soul to the Lord. Do not take your servant for a wicked woman; I have been praying here out of my great anguish and grief."

Eli answered, "Go in peace, and may the God of Israel grant you what you have asked of him."

She said, "May your servant find favor in your eyes." Then she went her way and ate something, and her face was no longer downcast.

Early the next morning they arose and worshiped before the Lord and then went back to their home at Ramah. Elkanah made love to his wife Hannah, and the Lord remembered her. So in the course of time Hannah became pregnant and gave birth to a son. She named him Samuel, saying, "Because I asked the Lord for him" (1 Samuel 1-20 NIV)

Hannah kept her promise to God and when Samuel was no longer a baby she brought him to the house of the Lord to live (1 Samuel 1 21-28 NIV)

The Shunammite Woman:

The Bible does not mention this woman's name. We only know that she was hospitable to the prophet Elisha.

One day Elisha went to Shunem. And a well-to-do woman was there, who urged him to stay for a meal. So whenever he came by, he stopped there to eat. She said to her husband, "I know that this man who often comes our way is a holy man of God. Let's make a small room on the roof and put in it a bed and a table, a chair and a lamp for him. Then he can stay there whenever he comes to us."

One day when Elisha came, he went up to his room and lay down there. He said to his servant Gehazi, "Call the Shunammite." So he called her, and she stood before him. Elisha said to him, "Tell her, 'You have gone to all this trouble for us. Now what can be done for you? Can we speak on your behalf to the king or the commander of the army?'"

She replied, "I have a home among my own people."

"What can be done for her?" Elisha asked.

Gehazi said, "She has no son, and her husband is old."

Then Elisha said, "Call her." So he called her, and she stood in the doorway. "About this time next year," Elisha said, "you will hold a son in your arms."

"No, my lord!" she objected. "Please, man of God, don't mislead your servant!"

But the woman became pregnant, and the next year about that same time she gave birth to a son, just as Elisha had told her.

The child grew, and one day he went out to his father, who was with the reapers. He said to his father, "My head! My head!"

His father told a servant, "Carry him to his mother." After the servant had lifted him up and carried him to his mother, the boy sat on her lap until noon, and then he died. She went up and laid him on the bed of the man of God, then shut the door and went out.

She called her husband and said, "Please send me one of the servants and a donkey so I can go to the man of God quickly and return."

"Why go to him today?" he asked. "It's not the New Moon or the Sabbath."

"That's all right," she said.

She saddled the donkey and said to her servant, "Lead on; don't slow down for me unless I tell you." So she set out and came to the man of God at Mount Carmel.

When he saw her in the distance, the man of God said to his servant Gehazi, "Look! There's the Shunammite! Run to meet her and ask her, 'Are you all right? Is your husband all right? Is your child all right?'"

"Everything is alright," she said.

When she reached the man of God at the mountain, she took hold of his feet. Gehazi came over to push her away, but the man of God said, "Leave her alone! She is in bitter distress, but the Lord has hidden it from me and has not told me why."

"Did I ask you for a son, my lord?" she said. "Didn't I tell you, 'Don't raise my hopes'?"

Elisha said to Gehazi, "Tuck your cloak into your belt, take my staff in your hand and run. Don't greet anyone you meet, and if anyone greets you, do not answer. Lay my staff on the boy's face."

But the child's mother said, "As surely as the Lord lives and as you live, I will not leave you." So he got up and followed her.

46

Gehazi went on ahead and laid the staff on the boy's face, but there was no sound or response. So Gehazi went back to meet Elisha and told him, "The boy has not awakened."

When Elisha reached the house, there was the boy lying dead on his couch. He went in, shut the door on the two of them and prayed to the Lord. Then he got on the bed and lay on the boy, mouth to mouth, eyes to eyes, hands to hands. As he stretched himself out on him, the boy's body grew warm. Elisha turned away and walked back and forth in the room and then got on the bed and stretched out on him once more. The boy sneezed seven times and opened his eyes.

 Elisha summoned Gehazi and said, "Call the Shunammite." And he did. When she came, he said, "Take your son." She came in, fell at his feet and bowed to the ground. Then she took her son and went out" (2 Kings 4:8-36 NIV).

Elizabeth and Zechariah:

In the time of Herod king of Judea there was a priest named Zechariah, who belonged to the priestly division of Abijah; his wife Elizabeth was also a descendant of Aaron. Both of them were righteous in the sight of God, observing all the Lord's commands and decrees blamelessly. But they were childless because Elizabeth was not able to conceive, and they were both very old."

Once when Zechariah's division was on duty and he was serving as priest before God, he was chosen by lot, according to the custom of the priesthood, to go into the temple of the Lord and burn incense. And when the time for the burning of incense came, all the assembled worshipers were praying outside.

Then an angel of the Lord appeared to him, standing at the right side of the altar of incense. When Zechariah saw him, he was startled and was gripped with fear. But the angel said to him: "Do not be afraid, Zechariah; your prayer has been heard. Your wife Elizabeth will bear you a son, and you are to call him John. He will be a joy and delight to you, and many will rejoice because of his birth, for he will be great in the sight of the Lord. He is never to take wine or other fermented drink, and he will be filled with the Holy Spirit even before he is born. He will bring back many of the people of Israel to the Lord their God. And he will go on before the Lord, in the spirit and power of Elijah, to turn the hearts of the parents to their children and the disobedient to the wisdom of the righteous—to make ready a people prepared for the Lord."

Zechariah asked the angel, "How can I be sure of this? I am an old man and my wife is well along in years."

The angel said to him, "I am Gabriel. I stand in the presence of God, and I have been sent to speak to you and to tell you this good news. And now you will be silent and not able to speak until the day this happens, because you did not believe my words, which will come true at their appointed time."

Meanwhile, the people were waiting for Zechariah and wondering why he stayed so long in the temple. When he came out, he could not speak to them. They realized he had seen a vision in the temple, for he kept making signs to them but remained unable to speak.

When his time of service was completed, he returned home. After this his wife Elizabeth became pregnant and for five months remained in seclusion. "The Lord has done this for me," she said. "In these days he has shown his favor and taken away my disgrace among the people (Luke 1:5-25 NIV.)".

"Blessed is she who has believed that the Lord would fulfill his promises to her" - Luke 1:45

Reflective Notes